IT'S TIME TO LEARN ABOUT BOOMSLANGS

It's Time to Learn about Boomslangs

Walter the Educator

Silent King Books
A WhichHead Entertainment Imprint

Copyright © 2025 by Walter the Educator

All rights reserved. No part of this book may be reproduced in any manner whatsoever without written per- mission except in the case of brief quotations embodied in critical articles and reviews.

First Printing, 2024

Disclaimer

This book is a literary work; the story is not about specific persons, locations, situations, and/or circumstances unless mentioned in a historical context. Any resemblance to real persons, locations, situations, and/or circumstances is coincidental. This book is for entertainment and informational purposes only. The author and publisher offer this information without warranties expressed or implied. No matter the grounds, neither the author nor the publisher will be accountable for any losses, injuries, or other damages caused by the reader's use of this book. The use of this book acknowledges an understanding and acceptance of this disclaimer.

It's Time to Learn about Boomslangs is a collectible early learning book by Walter the Educator suitable for all ages belonging to Walter the Educator's Time to Eat Book Series. Collect more books at WaltertheEducator.com

USE THE EXTRA SPACE TO TAKE NOTES AND DOCUMENT YOUR MEMORIES

BOOMSLANGS

Deep in the trees, so green and long,

It's Time to Learn about
Boomslangs

Slithers a snake both fast and strong.

With scales so smooth in shades so bright,

It hides by day and hunts at night.

The Boomslang's colors change and shine,

From leafy green to dark design.

Some are yellow, some are brown,

Blending in and slinking down.

Its body's thin, its eyes so wide,

Watching all as it glides.

With a flick of tongue, it smells the air,

To find its food just hiding there.

High in the trees, it moves with ease,

Balancing lightly in the breeze.

It twists, it turns, it climbs up high,

Almost like it learns to fly!

It's Time to Learn about
Boomslangs

The Boomslang waits, so still, so sly,

It watches birds and lets them fly.

Then with a strike so quick and neat,

It grabs its prey, it's time to eat!

But don't you fear, it's shy and small,

It won't attack, no, not at all!

Unless disturbed, it stays away,

And hides among the leaves all day.

Its venom works, but oh, so slow,

A single bite, and then you'll know.

But Boomslangs use their fangs with care,

Only when they must beware.

With fangs set far, not at the front,

It's not like snakes that strike and hunt.

Its poison helps it catch its food,

It's Time to Learn about
Boomslangs

But never harms if left unpursued.

Through forests bright and sunny skies,

The Boomslang slinks with clever eyes.

It helps to keep the balance right,

By hunting pests both day and night.

So if you see this snake so grand,

Just watch it move across the land.

A Boomslang's smart, a jungle king,

It's Time to Learn about
Boomslangs

A snake that climbs and makes life sing!

ABOUT THE CREATOR

Walter the Educator is one of the pseudonyms for Walter Anderson. Formally educated in Chemistry, Business, and Education, he is an educator, an author, a diverse entrepreneur, and he is the son of a disabled war veteran.
"Walter the Educator" shares his time between educating and creating. He holds interests and owns several creative projects that entertain, enlighten, enhance, and educate, hoping to inspire and motivate you. Follow, find new works, and stay up to date with Walter the Educator™

at WaltertheEducator.com

www.ingramcontent.com/pod-product-compliance
Lightning Source LLC
LaVergne TN
LVHW051919060526
838201LV00060B/4077